PIANO | VOCAL | GUITAR

THE BEST OF
STEVIE WONDER

Cover Photo: Black Star/Picturequest

ISBN 978-0-634-03164-9

HAL•LEONARD®
CORPORATION

7777 W. BLUEMOUND RD. P.O. BOX 13819 MILWAUKEE, WI 53213

Visit Hal Leonard Online at
www.halleonard.com

EBONY AND IVORY

Words and Music by
McCARTNEY

FINGERTIPS (PART 2)

Words and Music by CLARENCE O. PAUL
and HENRY COSBY

Solo ends I know that I nev - er gon - na hey, yeah. _ Ev - 'ry -

bod - y had a good time. __ So if you want me to, if you want me to; I'm gon-na

swing this song, __ yeah, just a one more time __ un - til I come back, _

__ just a one more time __ when I come back. __ So be ad - vised. *Harmonica solo*

Cm

FOR ONCE IN MY LIFE

Words by RONALD MILLER
Music by ORLANDO MURDEN

HIGHER GROUND

Words and Music by
STEVIE WONDER

I JUST CALLED TO SAY I LOVE YOU

Words and Music by
STEVIE WONDER

Additional Lyrics

3. No summer's high; no warm July;
   No harvest moon to light one tender August night.
   No autumn breeze; no falling leaves;
   Not even time for birds to fly to southern skies.

4. No Libra sun; no Halloween;
   No giving thanks to all the Christmas joy you bring.
   But what it is, though old so new
   To fill your heart like no three words could ever do.

I WISH

Words and Music by
STEVIE WONDER

Looking back on when _____ I was a little nap-py head-ed boy. ___
Broth-er says he's tell - in' 'bout you play - in' doc - tor with __ that girl. ___

I WAS MADE TO LOVE HER

Words and Music by STEVIE WONDER,
LULA MAE HARDAWAY, SYLVIA MOY and HENRY COSBY

I was born in Li'l Rock,   had a child-hood sweet-heart;
been my in-spi-ra-tion,   showed ap-pre-ci-a-tion
My ba-by loves me,   my ba-by needs me and I

we were al-ways hand in hand.   I wore high
for the love I gave her through the years.   Like a sweet
know I ain't go-ing no-where.   I was knee-

IF YOU REALLY LOVE ME

Words and Music by STEVIE WONDER
and SYREETA WRIGHT

If you real-ly love me, if you real-ly love me,

if you real-ly love me won't you tell me? Then,

I __ won't have _ to be __ play-ing a - round. __

You call my
I see the

ISN'T SHE LOVELY

Words and Music by
STEVIE WONDER

LIVING FOR THE CITY

Words and Music by
STEVIE WONDER

Moderate 4

A boy is born ___ in hard time Mis-sis-sip-pi,
His fa-ther works ___ some days for four-teen hours, ___
His sis-ter's black ___ but she is sho 'nuff pret-ty.
Her broth-er's smart, ___ he's got more sense than man-y.

sur-round-ed by ___ four walls that ain't so pret-ty. ___
and you can bet ___ he bare-ly makes a dol-lar. ___
Her skirt is short, ___ but Lord her legs are stur-dy. ___
His pa-tience's long, ___ but soon he won't have an-y. ___

His par-ents give ___ him
His moth-er goes ___ to
To walk to school, ___ she's
To find a job ___ is

*Original key: Gb major. This edition has been transposed up one half-step to be more playable.

MY CHERIE AMOUR

Words and Music by STEVIE WONDER,
SYLVIA MOY and HENRY COSBY

SIGNED, SEALED, DELIVERED I'M YOURS

Words and Music by STEVIE WONDER, SYREETA WRIGHT,
LEE GARRETT and LULA MAE HARDAWAY

Like a fool I went and stayed _ too long. _ Now I'm won - d'rin' if _ your love's
Then that time I went and said _ good-bye. _ Now I'm back _ and not _ a-shamed
Seen a lot of things in this _ old world. _ When I touched _ them they _ did noth -
Ooh-wee babe, you set my world _ on fire. _ That's why I know you're my one and on -

still strong. _
to cry. _
ing, girl. _   } Oo   ba - by,   here I am, _ signed, sealed, de-liv-ered I'm yours. _
ly de-sire. _

Here I am,

CODA

A PLACE IN THE SUN

Words and Music by RONALD MILLER
and BRYAN WELLS

RIBBON IN THE SKY

Words and Music by
STEVIE WONDER

Oh, so

SIR DUKE

Words and Music by
STEVIE WONDER

SUPERSTITION

Words and Music by
STEVIE WONDER

Ver - y su - per - sti -

D.S. al Coda

CODA

Su - per - sti - tion ain't the way. _____

(vocal 1st time only)

Repeat and Fade

Optional Ending

UPTIGHT
(Everything's Alright)

Words and Music by STEVIE WONDER,
SYLVIA MOY and HENRY COSBY

Lyrics:

Ba - by, ev - 'ry-thing is all right, up-tight, out __ of sight. __

Ba - by, ev - 'ry-thing is all right, up-tight, out __ of sight. __ I'm a

poor man's son __ from a-cross the rail-road tracks. __ The on - ly shirt I own is hang
no one __ is bet - ter than I. I know I'm __ just an

YOU AND I

Words and Music by
STEVIE WONDER

YOU ARE THE SUNSHINE OF MY LIFE

Words and Music by
STEVIE WONDER

YOU HAVEN'T DONE NOTHIN'

Words and Music by
STEVIE WONDER

tell - in' how you are gon - na change right from wrong.
tell - in' us how you are chang - ing right from wrong.

Bb7   Ebm7   D7   Db7   C7#9   B7   Bb7sus

'Cause if you real - ly want to hear our views,

Ebm7

you have - n't done _ noth - in'.

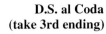